SEPHARIAL'S BOOK OF

CHARMS AND
TALISMANS

SEPHARIAL'S BOOK OF

CHARMS AND TALISMANS

foulsham

LONDON • NEW YORK • TORONTO • SYDNEY

foulsham

Yeovil Road, Slough, Berkshire SL1 4JH

ISBN 0–572–01544–5
Copyright © 1989   W. Foulsham and Co. Ltd

Printed in Great Britain at St Edmundsbury Press
Bury St Edmunds

CONTENTS

PREFACE

Probably from the dawn of time, and certainly from the earliest civilisations, people have been intrigued by the mysteries of the universe and scholars throughout the ages have devoted themselves to learning the secrets of occult influences which affect life on this earth. From the knowledge gained, these Ancients were able to devise charms (amulets) and talismans embodying the power to afford protection or bring good fortune to the wearer.

No one in modern times has made a more profound study or gained greater knowledge of these matters than Sepharial. His earlier work on this subject was closely related to the science of astrology. The present volume is written for the reader with little or no astrological knowledge. Its fascinating history of charms and talismans will show how our present-day lucky charms have come about, whilst guidance is given for those who wish to make their own talismans.

A special section is also included on the use of crystals and precious stones, which have become a popular form of talismanic tool for the occultist in recent times.

CHAPTER 1

HISTORY AND BACKGROUND

Numbers in some degree provide the mysticism and the potency of almost every charm and talisman. Most of the known talismans and charms come out of the numbers and symbols of the ancient languages— Hebrew, Sanskrit, Chinese, Egyptian and so on. We all know of the tremendous force which lies behind the swastika and the potency of the Egyptian scarab.

Pythagoras and Plato both understood the power of numbers and the magic in the world of their day, some 500 years before Christ. They knew the value of sound, form and colour and out of the studies of these Masters of Arts of past times come the present-day charm and talisman.

The ancient magicians, for example, knew that black and white stood symbolically for life and death, yellow and orange signified intuition, red was for life and passion, and blue for intellect. From ancient times all magicians have made use of colour and the vibrational numerical power of names in order to carry out their Talismanic Art. This is the reason why talismans embody numbers, symbols and signs of a language.

People who carry a mascot, such as a jewelled Egyptian scarab or a sapphire in a mounted or en-

11

graved gold ring are following the same kind of belief as the person who walks out into the road to avoid going under a ladder. Some of these people go so far, in the event of their being compelled to walk under the ladder, as to keep the first and second fingers crossed, the first finger being the finger linked with Providence and Protection and the second with Fate or Misfortune, until they meet a dog (a good portent, since dog is the friend of man). Keeping the fingers crossed is one form of ancient voodoo for averting the evil eye, or the villain.

Then we have the individual who wears a talisman in order to tone up the mental faculties and thus create self-confidence in all the daily tasks encountered in everyday life. He or she is invoking a good force that will help to overcome problems.

Few people indeed are ever inspired to wear evil talismans on their persons and this takes us back to the philosophers of the early days who were always thinking in terms of goodness in life—Christianity as we know it today—and the overcoming of evil forces of the world through good influences.

The Significance of Numbers

The Number 1 is the number of Unity. It represents the source of all creation, is indicative of the Divine Being and is the symbol of the Supreme Will in action.

The Number 2 is the number of Duality. It represents the blending of the masculine and feminine principles and is associated with the dual functions of Spirit and Matter, of the visible and invisible worlds.

The Number 3 is the number of the Trinity. It represents Spirit, Soul and Body. It is a very powerful number, associated at times with marriage and sex, and with the offspring. Wisdom, Love and Truth are three of its tenets.

The Number 4 denotes solidity and the material world and is often associated with the Cross, with the four seasons of the year, with the four suits in cards. Intellectually it denotes the realising of desires and wishes as a result of affirmation, plus emotional intensity and ardour.

The Number 5 is the number of Man. It is connected with the Pentagram or five-pointed star which in itself is the symbol of man or woman with arms outstretched and feet firmly placed on the earth, with head and eyes looking upward to heaven.

The Number 6 is the number that shows the dividing path of Virtue and Vice. It signifies the strife between conscience and passion, the choice between the two paths of good and evil. It denotes the antagonism of natural forces.

The Number 7 is often termed the 'Mystic Number' and is frequently used in magical ceremonies and rituals. It shows the domination of both the seen and the unseen by the power of the will and in the magical world the controlling of the four elements of Fire, Earth, Air and Water by the soul or astral counterpart of the human being.

The Number 8 is the number of Justice or Equilibrium. It is associated with both the destruction and reconstruction of natural things. It shows life in its fullness and is connected with the moment of death.

The Number 9 is the number of experience. It portrays knowledge of the past, present and future and is often called the number of 'The Hidden Light'. It symbolises both science and the magical art in combination.

The Number 10 is the number of Destiny. It shows changes which can be either good or bad: a sudden raising to a high position or equally as suddenly a loss of position and a personal downfall, dependent in many ways upon the previous action of the person concerned.

The Number 11 is the number of transformation which can again be from bad to good or from good to bad according to the personal inclinations and actions.

The Number 12 is the number of the Philosopher's Stone, the number of Transmutation. It is associated with the process of turning base metals into gold or transmuting selfish principles of character into those of an unselfish nature.

The Number 13 is the number of Resurrection. Whilst associated to some extent with the condition of death it really shows the trend and development of affairs after death rather than of death itself which is ruled by the number 8.

The Number 14 is the number of the Union of Forces and Ideas and as it is composed of two sevens it helps in the understanding of natural science and of alchemy. The Elixir of Life is often associated with this number.

The Number 15 is the number of fatality and is connected with all forms of mystery, of the unknown and unforeseen, and of Black Magic. It is a number of great power and very seldom fully understood.

The Number 16 is the number of accident or catastrophe, in many instances brought on by personal recklessness or a refusal to look facts in the face. Yet it can bestow courage and enable progress to be made once there is a proper controlling of inner rebellion and resentment.

The Number 17 is a fortunate number. It gives inner illumination and is often associated with divination and prophecy. It brings a blending of reason with intuition and strengthens the principles of Truth, Hope and Faith.

The Number 18 on the other hand is the number of deception and sometimes of diabolical inspiration. It will bring personal temptations which will be very hard to resist and shows unhappiness through the unfaithfulness of others.

The Number 19 is a number associated with personal happiness. It has much to do with the affections and with friendships and associations and shows that correct companionship will aid the general progress in life.

The Number 20 is connected with the home and the domestic and family side of life. It indicates that a conscientious carrying out of duties and responsibilities in these directions will do much towards creating security during the latter part of life.

The Number 21 is another very powerful number as it comprises three sevens. It helps to bring success and attainment providing the requisite effort is put forth and there is a retaining of a proper sense of proportion and perspective.

The Number 22 is one of the worst numbers. It shows a danger or failure usually through a blindness to face up to the facts of any given situation and a taking of things too much for granted.

The descriptions that have been given, although brief, can be associated with the number of one's name, with the number of a house, with the number of a year, even with the registered number of a Company and if any of these numbers are of a total of over 22 the key number can be obtained by adding the units of a number together until they reach 22 or under. Thus if a number is say—1298—then the units would be added together thus:

$$1 + 2 + 9 + 8 = 20$$

and this would be the basic number. If the number should be 1998, the units would be added as $1 + 9 + 9 + 8 = 27$ and, as this total exceeds 22, it would be further reduced by adding $2 + 7$, providing the basic number 9.

In general, the units from 1 to 9 are associated with divine principles; the tens, 10 to 90, are associated with Intellectual principles. The hundreds, 100 to 900 are connected with psychic and emotional factors, whilst the thousands, from 1000 onwards are connected with the material interests of life.

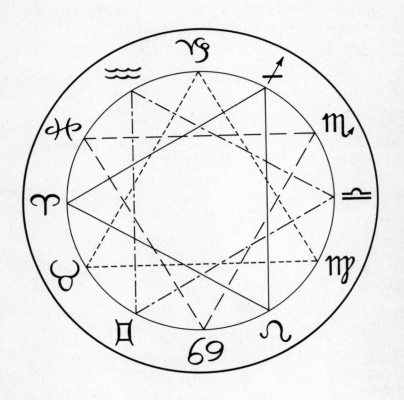

CHAPTER 2

NUMBERS AND THEIR SIGNIFICANCE

Each number has a variety of attributes and meanings and is associated with various factors such as a specific letter of the alphabet, a principle of character, a planetary or zodiacal association, a metal or precious stone, a colour and a divinatory signification.

The alphabetical letter although given in English is derived from the Hebrew alphabet which has twenty-two letters against the twenty-six of the English alphabet. Thus it will be seen that the number 3 is given the Kabalistic letter of G which is the third letter of the Hebrew alphabet and not the letter C which is the third letter of the English alphabet. Other variations and distinctions will be noted in this alphabetical distribution, but remember that we are dealing with magical principles; principles which throughout the ages have been used in the making of charms and talismans, and these principles supersede the distinctions of the alphabet.

The divinatory significations are linked with the Egyptian Tarot and in particular with the 22 Major Arcana of the Tarot which in turn are linked with the 22 letters of the Hebrew alphabet.

Each number has a divine, an intellectual, an

emotional and a material attribute and these are given
with their ancient meanings as follows:

The Number 1

The Kabalistic Letter is A.
The Divine Principle is Over-all Dominion.
The Intellectual Attribute is Austerity.
The Emotional Attribute is Selfishness.
The Material Factor is Bureaucracy.
The Planetary Association is the planet Mercury (☿).
The Appropriate Metal is Quicksilver.
The Vibratory Colour is Grey.
The Divinatory or Tarot Signification
(Arcanum I The Magician) denotes Will—Dexterity.

The Number 2

The Kabalistic Letter is B.
The Divine Principle is the Manifestation in Material
    Form of Spiritual Conceptions.
The Intellectual Attribute is The Analysing of
    Thought Processes.
The Emotional Attribute is Calmness.
The Material Factor is Ambition.
The Zodiacal Association is the sign Virgo (♍).
The Appropriate Stones are Pink Jasper, Hyacinth.
The Vibratory Colour is Dark Blue striped with White.
The Divinatory or Tarot Signification
(Arcanum II Veiled Isis) denotes Science.

The Number 3

The Kabalistic Letter is G.
The Divine Principle is Forgiveness.
The Intellectual Attribute is Understanding.
The Emotional Attribute is Tenderness.
The Material Factor is Enjoyment or Luxury.
The Zodiacal Association is the sign Libra (♎).
The Appropriate Stones are the Diamond and Opal.
The Vibratory Colour is Dark Blue or Ultramarine.
The Divinatory or Tarot Signification
(Arcanum III Isis Unveiled) denotes Marriage or
   Action.

The Number 4

The Kabalistic Letter is D.
The Divine Principle is Wisdom.
The Intellectual Attribute is Absorption of
   Knowledge.
The Emotional Attribute is Pride.
The Material Factor is Continuity of Effort.
The Zodiacal Association is the sign Scorpio (♏).
The Appropriate Stones are the Carbuncle and
   Turquoise.
The Vibratory Colour is Yellow tinged with Red.
The Divinatory or Tarot Signification
(Arcanum IV The Sovereign) denotes Realisation.

The Number 5

The Kabalistic Letter is E.
The Divine Principle is Reflection.
The Intellectual Attribute is Reverie.
The Emotional Attribute is Repose.
The Material Factor is Idleness.
The Planetary Association is the planet Jupiter (4).
The Appropriate Metal is Tin.
The Vibratory Colour is Purple.
The Divinatory or Tarot Signification
(Arcanum V The Hierophant) denotes 'Religion or
    Law.

The Number 6

The Kabalistic Letters are U.V.W.
The Divine Principle is Intuition.
The Intellectual Attribute is Aspiration.
The Emotional Attribute is Self-indulgence.
The Material Factor is Independence.
The Planetary Association is the planet Venus ($♀$).
The Appropriate Metal is Copper.
The Vibratory Colour is Blue.
The Divinatory or Tarot Signification
(Arcanum VI The Two Paths) denotes Temptation.

The Number 7

The Kabalistic Letter is Z.

The Divine Principle is The Triumph of Good over Evil.

The Intellectual Attribute is Applied Knowledge.

The Emotional Attribute is Righteous Anger.

The Material Factor is Conquest.

The Zodiacal Association is the sign Sagittarius (♐).

The Appropriate Stones are the Jasper and Malachite.

The Vibratory Colour is Crimson or Blood Red.

The Divinatory or Tarot Signification

(Arcanum VII The Conqueror) denotes Victory.

The Number 8

The Kabalistic Letter is H.

The Divine Principle is Justice.

The Intellectual Attribute is Calculation.

The Emotional Attribute is Equilibrium.

The Material Factor is the Balance between Greed and Improvidence.

The Zodiacal Association is the sign Capricorn (♑).

The Appropriate Stones are the White Onyx and the Moon Stone.

The Vibratory Colour is Dark Brown streaked with White.

The Divinatory or Tarot Signification

(Arcanum VIII The Balance) denotes Justice and Equilibrium.

The Number 9

The Kabalistic Letter is Th.
The Divine Principle is Prudence.
The Intellectual Attribute is Analysis.
The Emotional Attribute is Fear.
The Material Factor is Caution.
The Zodiacal Association is the sign Aquarius (≈).
The Appropriate Stone is the Sapphire.
The Vibratory Colour is Blue with White.
The Divinatory or Tarot Signification
(Arcanum IX The Sage) denotes Wisdom or
    Prudence.

The Number 10

The Kabalistic Letters are I.J.Y.
The Divine Principle is Faith.
The Intellectual Attribute is Learning.
The Emotional Attribute is Self-confidence.
The Material Factor is Self-preservation.
The Planetary Association is the planet Uranus (⛢).
The Appropriate Metal is Uranium.
The Vibratory Colour is Black or Brown and White
    Check.
The Divinatory or Tarot Signification
(Arcanum X The Wheel) denotes Changes of Fortune.

The Number 11

The Kabalistic Letters are C. K.
The Divine Principle is Fortitude.
The Intellectual Attribute is Continuity.
The Emotional Attribute is Sympathy.
The Material Factor is Persistence.
The Planetary Association is the Planet Neptune (Ψ).
The Appropriate Metal is Helium.
The Vibratory Colour is Mauve.
The Divinatory or Tarot Signification
(Arcanum XI The Enchantress) denotes Spiritual
   Power or Fortitude.

The Number 12

The Kabalistic Letter is L.
The Divine Principle is Compassion.
The Intellectual Attribute is Investigation.
The Emotional Attribute is Patience.
The Material Factor is Indifference to the Vicissitudes
   of Fate.
The Zodiacal Association is the sign Pisces ($\mathbf{H}$).
The Appropriate Stones are the White Chrysolite and
   Moonstone.
The Vibratory Colour is Dazzling White.
The Divinatory or Tarot Signification
(Arcanum XII The Martyr) denotes Sacrifice or Ex-
   piation.

The Number 13

The Kabalistic Letter is M.
The Divine Principle is Hope.
The Intellectual Attribute is Inspiration.
The Emotional Attribute is Devotion.
The Material Factor is Reconstruction.
The Zodiacal Association is the sign Aries (♈).
The Appropriate Stones are the Amethyst and the Diamond.
The Vibratory Colour is Red and White.
The Divinatory or Tarot Signification
(Arcanum XIII The Reaper) denotes Death or Transformation.

The Number 14

The Kabalistic Letter is N.
The Divine Principle is Toleration.
The Intellectual Attribute is Moderation.
The Emotional Attribute is Temperance.
The Material Factor is Vacillation.
The Zodiacal Association is the sign Taurus (♉).
The Appropriate Stones are the Moss Agate and the Emerald.
The Vibratory Colour is Greenish Yellow or Russet.
The Divinatory or Tarot Signification
(Arcanum XIV The Alchemist) denotes Regeneration or Temperance.

The Number 15

The Kabalistic Letter is X.
The Divine Principle is Predestination.
The Intellectual Attribute is Eloquence.
The Emotional Attribute is Sadness.
The Material Factor is Fatality.
The Planetary Association is the planet Saturn (♄).
The Appropriate Metal is Lead.
The Vibratory Colour is Black.
The Divinatory or Tarot Signification
(Arcanum XV The Black Magician) denotes Fatality
    or Black Magic.

The Number 16

The Kabalistic Letter is O.
The Divine Principle is Godly Fear.
The Intellectual Attribute is Study.
The Emotional Attribute is Belief.
The Material Factor is Hard Work.
The Planetary Association is the planet Mars (♂).
The Appropriate Metal is Iron.
The Vibratory Colour is Red.
The Divinatory or Tarot Signification
(Arcanum XVI The Lightning Flash) denotes
    Accident or Catastrophe.

The Number 17

The Kabalistic Letters are F. P.
The Divine Principle is Immortality.
The Intellectual Attribute is Expression of Ideas.
The Emotional Attribute is Expression of Beauty in Form.
The Material Factor is Artistic Creation.
The Zodiacal Association is the sign Gemini (♊).
The Appropriate Stones are the Beryl and Aquamarine.
The Vibratory Colour is Pink.
The Divinatory or Tarot Signification
(Arcanum XVII The Star) denotes Truth, Hope, Faith.

The Number 18

The Kabalistic Letter is Ts or Tz.
The Divine Principle is Universal Understanding.
The Intellectual Attribute is Mental Reflection.
The Emotional Attribute is Reaction.
The Material Factor is a danger of Wrong Action.
The Zodiacal Association is the sign Cancer (♋).
The Appropriate Stones are the Emerald and the Black Onyx.
The Vibratory Colour is Bright Green.
The Divinatory or Tarot Signification
(Arcanum XVIII The Moon) denotes Deception, False Friends, Secret Foes.

The Number 19

The Kabalistic Letter is Q.
The Divine Principle is Universal Religion.
The Intellectual Attribute is Reason.
The Emotional Attribute is Vanity.
The Material Factor is Progress through Effort.
The Zodiacal Association is the sign Leo (♌).
The Appropriate Stones are the Ruby and Diamond.
The Vibratory Colour is Fiery Red or Vermillion.
The Divinatory or Tarot Signification
(Arcanum XIX The Sun) denotes Happiness or Joy.

The Number 20

The Kabalistic Letter is R.
The Divine Principle is Eternal Life.
The Intellectual Attribute is Study of Philosophy.
The Emotional Attribute is Impulse.
The Material Factor is Responsibility.
The Planetary Association is the Moon (☽).
The Appropriate Metal is Silver.
The Vibratory Colour is Sea Green.
The Divinatory or Tarot Signification
(Arcanum XX The Sarcophagus) denotes Awakening
    or Resurrection.

The Number 21

The Kabalistic Letters are S. Sh.
The Divine Principle is Continuity of Life.
The Intellectual Attribute is Dramatic Expression.
The Emotional Attribute is Sensation.
The Material Factor is Being in Command.
The Planetary Association is the Sun (☉).
The Appropriate Metal is Gold.
The Vibratory Colour is Orange.
The Divinatory or Tarot Signification
(Arcanum XXI The Adept) denotes Success or
    Attainment.

The Number 22

The Kabalistic Letter is T.
The Divine Principle is Infinity.
The Intellectual Attribute is Doubt.
The Emotional Attribute is Uncertainty.
The Material Factor is Lack of Progress.
The Planetary Association is the Earth (⊕).
The Appropriate Metal is—None—as the Earth con-
    tains all metals.
The Vibratory Colour is Green.
The Divinatory or Tarot Signification
(Arcanum XXII The Materialist) denotes Failure,
    Folly, Mistake.

CHAPTER 3

CHARMS TO WEAR

Charms to wear or to carry on the person can be roughly divided into three main classes:

(1) Charms which are made in the form of rings, brooches, bracelets, necklaces, bangles, etc., and which contain certain precious stones;

(2) Charms which are made solely of metal and which are engraved with various designs;

(3) Charms which are really talismans, drawn on parchment or paper, or even on the back of a mirror, the drawings consisting of specific symbols enclosed in the form of a square, circle, pentagram, hexagram or any other form specifically designed to enclose or contain a power that will operate for the benefit of the wearer.

The first two kinds are made so as to be worn on the person, the third is made so as to be carried in a wallet or handbag, as long as the charm is first of all placed in a suitable container which can be made of silk or similar material.

Charms Containing Precious Stones

As stated, these are usually incorporated in rings, etc., which can be made of platinum, gold or silver, but which should preferably be made of gold as the vibration of this metal is much more in accord with the basic purpose for which the charm is made.

Particular precious stones can bring either good luck or ill luck. Some are more favourably disposed towards certain persons than to others and, in distinguishing between these for our own purposes, there are two methods which can be adopted. The first is according to the date of the month in which the individual is born and the second is in accord with the day of the week.

The first choice is determined by the passage of the Sun through the twelve zodiacal signs and not by the calendar months. To say that you are born in January or June is not sufficient, as the zodiacal signs do not influence each month from the 1st to the 30th or 31st or, in the case of February, from the 1st to the 28th or 29th. There is an apparently arbitrary dividing line which must of necessity be taken into account and this can occur from the 20th to the 24th of the month according to the particular part of the year in which you happen to be born.

The zodiac commences with the sign Aries and the Sun occupies this sign from March 21st to April 20th.

The following table shows the date changes during the year:

Periods in which the Sun is in the various
Signs of the Zodiac

♈	Aries	March 21st to April 20th
♉	Taurus	April 21st to May 21st
♊	Gemini	May 22nd to June 21st
♋	Cancer	June 22nd to July 22nd
♌	Leo	July 23rd to Aug. 23rd
♍	Virgo	Aug. 24th to Sept. 23rd
♎	Libra	Sept. 24th to Oct. 23rd
♏	Scorpio	Oct. 24th to Nov. 22nd
♐	Sagittarius	Nov. 23rd to Dec. 21st
♑	Capricorn	Dec. 22nd to Jan. 20th
♒	Aquarius	Jan. 21st to Feb. 19th
♓	Pisces	Feb. 20th to March 20th

In Chapter 2 a description of the various numbers was given and certain of these numbers are connected with the signs of the zodiac; thus the Number 2 is associated with the sign Virgo and also with the precious stones, Pink Jasper and Hyacinth, therefore when you know your zodiacal sign according to the date of your birth and the appropriate number allotted to that sign you will also know the precious stones which accord to both date and sign and these stones will be the stones to use and to incorporate in the ring, brooch, or other ornament which you wish to use as a charm.

The zodiacal signs, associated numbers and stones are tabulated here:

Sign		Number	Stone
Aries	♈	13	Diamond
Taurus	♉	14	Emerald
Gemini	♊	17	Agate
Cancer	♋	18	Ruby
Leo	♌	19	Sardonyx
Virgo	♍	2	Sapphire
Libra	♎	3	Opal
Scorpio	♏	4	Topaz
Sagittarius	♐	7	Turquoise
Capricorn	♑	8	Garnet
Aquarius	♒	9	Amethyst
Pisces	♓	12	Bloodstone

The stones listed are not the only ones suitable for association with each zodiacal sign and as you also may not be aware of the colour and appearance of these stones a brief description is given of some of the principles associated with them.

Amber—is considered especially fortunate when worn as a necklace and being a yellow stone is most applicable to Leo people and will aid them in the furthering of their ambitions and as regards children.

Amethyst—is a kind of quartz and can have a purple, violet or mauve colouring. The purple or violet would also be applicable to Aries. It is linked with St Valentine and assists those who wear it to maintain faithfulness. It is also said to ward off drunkenness.

Aquamarine—a precious stone of bright blue or bright green colour. Assists the inspiration and is favourable for travellers as it helps to protect against accidents. Very applicable to Gemini people.

Beryl—a mineral of great hardness rather than a precious stone. It comes from yellow quartz and can be worn as a protection against evil gossip and rumour. It is again especially suitable for Gemini born people.

Bloodstone—is the emblem of courage, and soldiers of old wore it in battle, believing it had the power to stop bleeding. It is more suitable for men than women, but whoever wears it has a talisman for warding off disease and accidents. It is suitable for Pisces people.

Carbuncle—a dark red precious stone somewhat after the style of a Garnet. Is another helpful stone for warding off infectious and internal diseases. Will increase the feeling of self-confidence and the ability to fight through difficulties. It is particularly helpful for Scorpio born people.

Coral—although this is not a precious stone in the strict meaning of the word, it comes under the influence of the planet Venus and is especially favourable for Taurus and Libra born people. It promises a long and happy married life and though more particularly applicable to women it is also helpful for men. It protects children from evil influences and safeguards the teenager during the highly emotional period.

Cornelian—was considered an extremely powerful

talisman in Egypt, Arabia and Turkey, and one that was highly favourable to health, long life and good fortune. It can be worn by anyone, irrespective of the particular month of birth.

Diamond—this is a precious stone made of carbon, which gives off a sparkling quality. It is said to symbolise bravery and strength and is also one of the emblems of innocence. Those born under the signs Aries, Leo or Libra can wear it.

Emerald—this is a precious stone of the beryl type and is of a beautiful green colour. Is said to be good for the eyes. Worn by a woman it helps her to attract true love and worn by a man will attract a loving wife. Should it be given by one lover to another and the love between them grows cold then the colour of the stone will change from bright to dull. It is favourable for Taurus, Cancer and Pisces people to wear.

Garnet—in appearance somewhat like an inferior ruby. Invariably red in colour but can also be black, brown or green. Is said to ward off inflammatory diseases and to promote a healthy and cheery disposition. Will ensure constancy in friendship and love and is generally fortunate for Capricorn people.

Jacynth—is said to render its wearer extremely fascinating. It should always be set in gold and is especially favourable for Aquarian born people, but less fortunate for Taurus born.

Jasper—another mineral of quartz basis which can be almost any colour, although with white, yellow and pink somewhat more predominant. It is worn so as to safeguard one's personal independence and is said to bring inspirational warnings when there is any danger of unfair domination from other people. Very good for Virgo and Sagittarius people.

Malachite—a precious stone that can be either black or white. It is a stone favourable for sea travellers, explorers, missionaries and those who are adventurous. Applies more particularly to Sagittarius people.

Moss Agate—sometimes known as the Scotch Pebble—is a semi-precious stone which has bands of colour running through it, sometimes green or blue, sometimes yellow, sometimes brown or dark red. It is said to assist in the making and keeping of friends and is helpful to farmers and all those interested in agriculture, horticulture and floriculture. For Taurus people the Moss Agate with a dark blue band running through it would be favourable, whilst Gemini born people could also wear this stone if it has a yellow band running through it. A green band would be more favourable for Cancer born people and a brown or dark red band for Scorpio people.

Onyx—of which Sardonyx is a variety. Can be white or black, or have red or white or dark brown markings. Protects against the bites of snakes and venomous insects and assists in bringing marital happiness. Favours Cancer, Leo and Capricorn born people.

Opal—a cloudy white precious stone. When it catches the light it can flash with rainbow hues. It is, however, usually considered an unlucky stone and can interfere with love and marriage, the exception being for Libra and Scorpio born people. To these people it will help to give second sight or clairvoyance and will strengthen other psychic faculties.

Pearls—these have been deemed as inspirers of love and are supposed to possess the power of curing fevers and irritable tempers. They can be worn by almost any type with the exception of Aries and Virgo people.

Ruby—one of the most precious of all jewels with the exception of the Diamond. It has a very clear brilliance and is somewhat similar in its composition to the Sapphire. Sometimes it is a deep glowing red but it can range from pink to almost violet. It is another stone helping to create and to maintain friendship and to banish grief. Particularly applicable to Aries, Cancer and Aquarian people.

Sapphire—usually of a clear cornflower blue. A precious stone that is a symbol of purity and is very fortunate for engaged couples and true lovers. It assists in promoting peaceful and happy conditions and is very good for those born under Libra, Aquarius, and Virgo. It can aid in curing mental disorders.

Topaz—a transparent precious stone of a clear yellow colour, but at times can be yellowish-white, blue or even pink. It is akin in its influence to Amber and is said to ward off chest and rheumatic troubles. Favours Gemini, Leo, Scorpio and Libra born people.

Turquoise—a stone that is blue or blue-green in colour. It can be waxy, opaque or translucent in appearance and a great deal is said to depend upon the health of the person who wears it. It helps to protect from misfortune or danger but it would be unwise for another person to wear it should it be taken from the body of someone who dies. In that contingency it would be better to have it repolished and reset in a different form; for example, if it had been in a ring formerly, have it reset in a brooch. It is fortunate for both Scorpio and Sagittarius people.

So far as the effective working of charms, amulets, talismans and other magical devices are concerned this can be summed up as follows:

'When the soul of the world by its virtue, impregnates all things that are either naturally or artificially made, it infuses into these things certain celestial values which will be able to produce wonderful effects in the terrestrial or earth world, particularly when they are worn on the person in the form of a ring, bangle, bracelet, necklace or brooch, and also when they are conveniently rolled up and tied on, hung from the neck or attached in any way to the person or carried by the person. Their virtue is then impressed on the person by the contact and they affect body, soul and mind, changing sickness to health, timidity to courage, sadness to happiness, bad fortune to good luck.'

The principle is that the influence cannot work *unless some form of physical contact is established* between the stone, metal, talisman, etc., and the person for whom the charm has been made or who has purchased it or made it themselves.

Other Forms of Charms

In addition to precious stones set in rings, etc., there are charms made in differing shapes and designs.

An Anchor, which can be made of various metals but preferably of iron, is an emblem of hope and, as is only natural, is associated with the sea and with all things of a seafaring nature. As an emblem of hope it can be made in the form of a badge or a brooch usually with a blue or a sea-green background. It is a charm associated with the Moon and the sign Cancer and with Saturn and the sign Capricorn.

The Egyptians were well versed in all matters to do with lucky charms and among the most popular was the Cat, an animal of which the Egyptians thought very highly, particularly if it was black. Hence a **Black Cat** is considered lucky and badges and brooches of metal can be made in which the design or figure is of a black cat. Usually the metal so used is an alloy and is black enamelled. It comes very much under the influence of the signs Capricorn and Pisces.

Spiders and beetles, scorpions and other insects have also been used by the Egyptians for charms and for furthering magical processes. Spiders and beetles in certain instances are said to attract money whilst scorpions will put up a guard against enmity and can even destroy those who seek to do one an ill or evil turn. They are most associated with the signs of Virgo and Scorpio than with other signs.

The Caduceus, or winged wand with two snakes entwining the staff, of joint Egyptian/Hebrew origin, is a mascot for persons in the world of commerce and business. It helps to promote very good business deals, allays differences and misunderstandings and over-comes quarrels. It is associated more with the sign Gemini than with any other sign. It is also associated with the staff of Hermes, the Greek god, and has been adopted as a symbol of the healing professions.

The Scarab is another Egyptian Charm which, from time immemorial, has been prized by them as an emblem of the Great Creator of the Universe. It figures on all their ancient buildings, ruins and temples and has been discovered by the thousand in the tomb of Tutankhamen. It was worn by the living and placed in the graves of the dead. These charms are sold at a high price by the Egyptian dragomans and others as objects of great veneration and of undisputed value to tourists. It helps to keep away misfortune.

A Swallow Charm, particularly in silver, is also considered to be very lucky. In certain instances the birds themselves were induced to build in the eaves of houses as this was considered a very good omen for a house and its inmates.

Models of hands open or closed are a favourite means of protection against the evil eye. They should be made in pottery or bronze. Amongst the Arabs they are known as Fatima's Hand.

Amongst Grecian and Etruscan charms are the Lion, for strength and bravery, the Unicorn for justice, the Lamb and the Dove for peace.

An Acorn: Throughout the history of England since the days of the Norman Conquest it has been the custom for people to carry a dried acorn for the maintaining of youthfulness and vigour. It is supposed to have the effect of making a wayward lover repent and return to his or her jilted companion. It can be made of copper or tin, and worn irrespective of one's birth month.

Angle: A metal charm made of iron in the shape of an angle shaped like the letter L, increases the intellectual capacity and gives ability for writing and oratory. It can be worn irrespective of the month of birth.

Arrowheads have served as charms since ancient times. The earliest were made of flint, but modern ones can be made of gold or silver and can be worn by men as a badge or by women hung around the neck. Their chief use again is to ward off the evil eye and to protect the wearer from evil intentions. They are especially favourable for Cancer and Sagittarius people.

Axes: These are somewhat similar to arrowheads and have the same signification, but apply more to Aries and Libra people, who should wear them made of silver or white metal.

Bamboo and Serpent: This is a very old talisman and consists of a ring bearing a number of triangles, made of gold. Lying on the ring is a serpent crossed with a stick of bamboo bearing seven knots. These can also be of gold or of other metal if desired. The ring stands for eternity which, like the ring, never ends.

The triangles on the ring symbolise the Trinity. The seven-knotted bamboo stood for the seven degrees of learning which had to be acquired in olden times, and the serpent was an additional sign of wisdom. This talisman can therefore be worn to secure long life and to acquire knowledge, understanding and wisdom. It is especially applicable to Virgo and Capricorn people.

Cornucopia: Otherwise called the horn of plenty. This mascot consists of a curved horn out of which emerges an unlimited supply of fruit and flowers. It is symbolic of plenty and to wear this mascot made in gold or silver helps to ensure an abundance of wealth and prosperity. Very favourable for Virgo and Sagittarian people.

Fish: The symbol of the Fish has always been regarded as a sign of increase and wealth because of its remarkable fertility. It is cut out of gold or mother-of-pearl and used as a charm or pendant for good fortune. It is extremely helpful for Pisces born people.

Heart: To wear the heart as a mascot is a relic of the Egyptian idea which was that people's hearts were to be weighed at the resurrection and those proving satisfactory would be accepted into heaven. The more modern interpretation is that the heart is a symbol of true love and these mascots are given as a symbol of genuine affection. They should be made of gold and are very fortunate for Leo and Libra people.

Key: The Greek key which figures in so many patterns is a symbol of both life and knowledge. Sometimes the symbol is in the form of three keys standing for love, wealth and health. The keys are said to unlock the doors which lead to these conditions. They are very suitable for Virgo, Scorpio and Aquarius people, and should be made of gold, hardened steel or chromium-plated metal.

Knot: A knot stands for the joining of things and hence knots have long been used for symbols by lovers. Everyone is familiar with the true lovers' knot. It can be made of gold, silver or platinum and favours Gemini and Pisces people.

Ladybird: A charm in such a form is supposed to bring financial good fortune and should also be made of gold as a badge or brooch. It is very good for Taurus and Leo people.

Owl: The owl is a bird symbolising knowledge and common sense and can therefore be worn by those who are desirous of acquiring knowledge and who are interested in learning and education. It should be made of gold, silver or copper and will apply more particularly to Taurus, Virgo and Capricorn people.

Tau: This symbol is in universal use as a sacred emblem. The simplest form is of a vertical pillar surmounted by a horizontal pillar, a very old form of cross. It will ward off diseases of the skin and help to keep one pure in thought. Especially helpful for all who are interested in religious and welfare matters, medicine, nursing, etc., and should be worn by Virgo, Scorpio and Pisces people. Gold, silver or copper are suitable metals.

The Four-leaved Clover is a charm of Irish origin

and each leaf has a separate meaning. The first leaf on the left of the stalk helps to bring fame; the second, moving clockwise, assists in the obtaining of wealth;

the third to the right brings a faithful lover or sweetheart and the fourth, on the right of the stalk, brings robust health. This charm can be made of tin or alloy and enamelled green. It is chiefly associated with the signs Cancer and Pisces.

A Grasshopper, also made of tin or alloy and enamelled green is said to bring riches and wealth and is favourable to farmers and all who have to do with the land. It is connected with the sign Virgo.

The Horseshoe is a well-known bringer of luck and good fortune, but contrary to popular opinion, which says that the points of the shoe should be upwards so that the luck doesn't fall out, the points should really be downwards for the symbol is taken from the Moon's North and South Nodes, the North Node whose symbol is ☊ being the fortunate node and the bringer and maintainer of prestige and reputation, and the South Node whose symbol is ☋ bringing loss, misfortune, and a loss of prestige and reputation. It should be made of tin or alloy as it is under the influence of the planet Jupiter, the planet of luck, and associated with the sign Sagittarius.

One could go on enumerating designs and their meanings, but enough has been said on this point and we should now proceed to understand the part that specific metals play.

Magic Seal Charms Made of Metal

Magic Seal Charms are made of the metals related to the planets and the planetary rule is as follows: Sun, gold; Moon, silver; Mercury, silver, platinum or aluminium; Venus, copper; Mars, iron; Jupiter, tin; Saturn, lead; Uranus, uranium; Neptune, neptunium; Pluto, plutonium.

Of these, the Uranian, Neptunian and Plutonian metals do not come into operation and are not used for the purpose of charms.

In order to make a magic seal of metal, a piece of the appropriate metal, in the form of a square or circle should be obtained and on one side in the centre should be engraved the square of numbers within the circles, with the Hebrew characters; and on the other side the seal of the planet chosen, also in the circles.

The squares and seals of the Moon are given first. Those of the other planets are illustrated on pages 50 and 51.

The Magic Tables, Seals and Characters of the Planets, their Intelligence and Spirits.

Table of the Moon in her Compass.

37	78	29	70	21	62	13	54	5
6	38	79	30	71	22	63	14	46
47	7	39	80	31	72	23	55	15
16	48	8	40	81	32	64	24	56
57	17	49	9	41	73	33	65	25
26	58	18	50	1	42	74	34	66
67	27	59	10	51	2	43	75	35
36	68	19	60	11	52	3	44	76
77	28	69	20	61	12	53	4	45

The same in Hebrew.

ה	עז	כט	ע	כא	סב	יג	נד	ה
ו	לח	עט	ל	עא	כב	סג	יד	מו
יה	נה	כג	עב	לא	פ	רט	ז	מז
נו	כד	סד	לב	פא	מ	ה	סד	יך
כה	סה	לג	על	מא	ט	מט	יז	נז
סו	לד	עד	מב	א	נ	יח	נח	כו
לה	עה	מג	נא	י	נא	נט	כז	סז
עו	מר	ג	יא	אם	נא	יט	סח	לו
מה	ר	נ	כ	יבמא	ל	כנ	בח	עז

Seal or
Character of the Moon.

Character of the
Spirit of the Moon.

Of the Spirit of the Spirits
of the Moon.

Of the Intelligence of the Intelligences
of the Moon.

Magic Seals or Talismans.

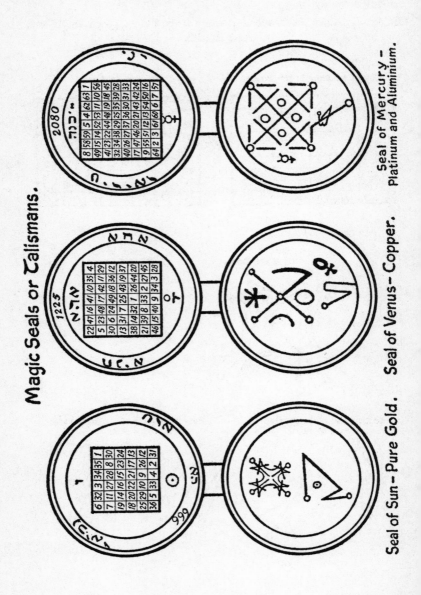

Seal of Sun – Pure Gold.   Seal of Venus – Copper.

Seal of Mercury –
Platinum and Aluminium.

Magic Seals or Talismans.

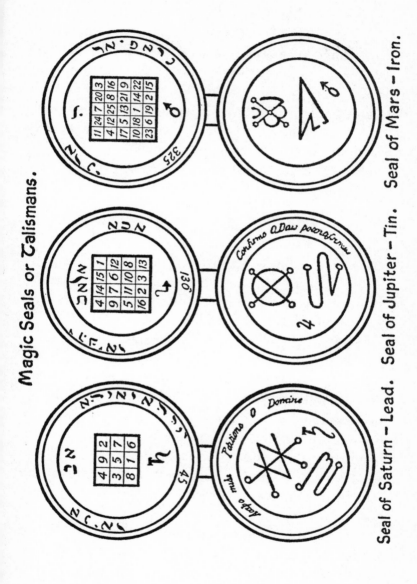

Seal of Saturn – Lead. Seal of Jupiter – Tin. Seal of Mars – Iron.

51

A brief explanation of these Tables shows that:

The Table of the Moon, ☽ , is a square of nine containing the numbers 1 to 81, each column vertically or horizontally, amounting to 369, the sum of all being 3,321.

The Table of the Sun, ☉ , is a square of six, containing numbers 1 to 36, the columns being each accounted 111, and the sum of all 666.

The Table of Mercury, ☿ , is a square of eight, containing 1 to 64, and each of its columns amounts to 260, the sum of all being 2,080.

The Table of Venus, ♀ , is a square of seven, containing 1 to 49, the columns amounting each to 175, and the sum of all to 1,225.

The Table of Mars, ♂ , is a square of five, containing numbers 1 to 25, the columns being each 65, and the sum of all 325.

The Table of Jupiter, ♃ , is a square of the Numbers 1 to 16, a square of four, the total of each column taken in any direction being 34, and the sum of all is 136.

The Table of Saturn, ♄ , consists of a square of three containing the numbers 1 to 9 disposed in such a manner that accounted vertically, horizontally, or diagonally, they add to 15, and the total of all the numbers is 45, which is expressed in the name of the Intelligence of Saturn, which is Agial.

The charms made of metal and engraved with the Tables and Seals of the planets can be used for certain specific purposes, thus:

If made of gold and engraved with the Table and Seal of the Sun it will help to promote good health, will create confidence in one's own abilities and draw out the power of leadership.

If made of silver and engraved with the Table and Seal of the Moon, it will aid in all things of an agricultural and domestic nature.

If made of silver, platinum or aluminium and engraved with the Table and Seal of Mercury it will aid in the acquiring and the expressing of knowledge and will assist in travel by road, rail and air.

If made of copper and engraved with the Table and Seal of Venus, it will assist all matters to do with the affections, with marriage, partnership, social and public affairs and with money.

If made with iron and engraved with the Table and Seal of Mars it will promote courage, physical strength and assist in the understanding of mechanics, of medicine and surgery and is good for the arts of war.

If made with tin and engraved with the Table and Seal of Jupiter it will attract Luck and Good Fortune, will exercise protection and will assist in commercial interests, legal matters, religious affairs, and is good for overseas travel.

If made of lead and engraved with the Table and Seal of Saturn it will strengthen the capacity to carry out duties and responsibilities; to take part in political and associated activities and to develop big business enterprises.

Metal charms made of gold will be especially favourable for people born July 23rd–August 23rd who come under the influence of the sign Leo, and its Ruler the Sun. The charm should follow the design as shown on page 50.

The Moon Table and seal shown on page 49 will be favourable for Cancer people—June 22nd–July 22nd.

For people born May 22nd–June 21st and August 24th–September 23rd under the influence of the signs Gemini and Virgo respectively with the planet Mercury as Ruler, the charm should be made of silver, platinum or aluminium, as these metals are ruled by Mercury. The diagram of Mercury is shown on page 50.

Charms made of copper will be fortunate for people born April 21st–May 21st under the influence of the sign Libra as both these signs are ruled by the planet Venus. The diagram for the Venus charm and Seal is shown on page 50.

People born under the influence of the planet Mars which rules the period March 21st–April 20th under the influence of the sign Aries, and the period October 24th–November 22nd under the influence of the sign Scorpio should wear charms made of iron bearing the Mars design as shown on page 51.

Charms made of tin will be favourable for people ruled by Jupiter, periods November 23rd–December 21st, sign Sagittarius, and February 20th–March 20th, sign Pisces. The diagram for Jupiter is shown on page 51.

Lead charms are favourable for people born under the influence of the planet Saturn, ruling from December 22nd–January 20th, Capricorn, and January 21st–February 19th, Aquarius. The diagram for the Saturn charm is given on page 51.

These charms should be made or bought as far as possible on the day ruled by the birth planet as shown hereunder, and in either the first, eighth, fifteenth or twenty-second hour of the day, as these are the hours ruled by the planet ruling the day.

Planet	Day
Sun	Sunday
Moon	Monday
Mars	Tuesday
Mercury	Wednesday
Jupiter	Thursday
Venus	Friday
Saturn	Saturday

The days of the week influence can also be applied to the choice and wearing of precious stones listed earlier in this chapter.

For people born on Sunday, the stones that are ruled by the sign Leo should be chosen. Those born on a Monday should choose stones ruled by the sign Cancer. People born on Tuesday should wear stones ruled by the sign Aries or Scorpio, those born in the positive hours, 1, 3, 5 and so on choosing Aries, and those born in the negative hours 2, 4, 6, etc., choosing

Scorpio. Do not forget that the first hour of the day is from 0 a.m. to 1 a.m. which would be positive, and the second hour from 1 a.m. to 2 a.m. which would be negative.

The same principle will apply to all the other days and planets. People born on a Wednesday should choose Gemini or Virgo stones, Gemini if born in a positive hour, Virgo if born in a negative hour. Thursday born people should wear Sagittarius or Pisces stones, Sagittarius if born in a positive hour, Pisces if born in a negative hour. Friday people should wear Libra or Taurus stones, Libra stones if born in a positive hour, Taurus if born in a negative hour. Saturday people should wear Capricorn or Aquarius stones, Aquarius if born in a positive hour and Capricorn if born in a negative hour.

The third class of charm is more distinctively known as a talisman which may be drawn on parchment or paper and can follow the same lines as those of the planets engraved on metal.

The metal charms can be worn as badges or brooches but the parchment or paper talismans should be placed in a wallet or silk bag, carried in the pocket or handbag or hung round the neck.

A fuller description of these will be given in subsequent chapters.

The following old doggerel serves as a general reminder of one's lucky birthstone; but as explained elsewhere, a further distinction should be made according to the actual date of birth in each month.

JANUARY

By her who in this month was born
No gem save Garnets should be worn—
They will insure her constancy,
True friendship, and fidelity.

FEBRUARY

The February born shall find
Sincerity and peace of mind,
Freedom from passion and from care
If they the Amethyst will wear.

MARCH

Who on this world of ours their eyes
In March first open shall be wise,
In days of peril, firm and brave,
And wear a Bloodstone to their grave.

APRIL

She who from April dates her years—
Diamonds should wear lest bitter tears
For vain repentance flow; this stone
Emblem of innocence is known.

MAY

Who first beholds the light of day
In spring's sweet, flowery month of May,
And wears an Emerald all her life
Shall be a loved and happy wife.

JUNE

Who comes with summer to this earth,

And owes to June her hour of birth,
With ring of Agate on her hand
Can health, wealth, and long life command.

JULY

The glowing Ruby shall adorn
Those who in warm July are born,
Then will they be exempt and free
From love's doubt and anxiety.

AUGUST

Wear a Sardonyx or for thee
No conjugal felicity—
The August born without this stone,
'Tis said, must live unloved and lone.

SEPTEMBER

A maiden born when autumn leaves
Are rustling in the September breeze,
A Sapphire on her brow should bind,
'Twill cure diseases of the mind.

OCTOBER

October child is born for woe,
And life's vicissitudes must know;
But lay an Opal on her breast,
And hope will lull those woes to rest.

NOVEMBER

Who first comes to this world below
With drear November's fog and snow
Should prize the Topaz's amber hue,

Emblem of friends and lovers true.

DECEMBER

If cold December gave you birth,
The month of snow and ice and mirth,
Place on your hand a Turquoise blue,
Success will bless whate'er you do.

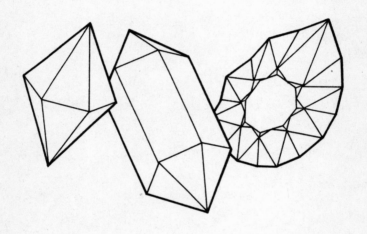

CHAPTER 4

BACKGROUND TO TALISMANS

People are often amused by seeing in the shops figures of human beings and of animals made of sweets or chocolate or of composite figures partly human and partly animal, and seldom stop to think that there can be any possible connection between this kind of confectionery and the varied forms of charms and talismans made of metals and precious stones. Yet there is a link and the sweet or chocolate figure perpetrates, from a very broad standpoint, images of ancient origin—Egyptian, Hebrew and others.

The totem poles of various tribes developed into the animal-headed gods of Egypt, suggesting that the god who began existence as an animal, bird or even insect, was endowed with a human intelligence although preserving the other characteristics as shown by the nature of his or her head.

A god of human form but with the head of an Ibis signified a god of Wisdom. The hawk head of Horus denoted his ability to soar supremely over all others.

Talismans made in these and other forms were worn both as a protection against evil and to assist in the attracting of brighter and happier conditions of life. The use of talismans against evil came first, and in ancient times the favourite jewels of an individual, which would include some of these talismans, would be buried with him (or her) after he had died so that the protective vibration could be maintained and assist him in his journey through the underworld, the astral and the spiritual planes. Sometimes, in the effort to ensure that the spirit of the individual would have sufficient nourishment to sustain him on his journey, the outline of a leg of beef would be carved upon the wall of the tomb so as to enable the spirit of the individual to live upon the spirit of the beef.

From another standpoint, the principle of protection was invoked by the drawing of certain hieroglyphics such as a lion, a horned viper, a long winding snake and a bee, minus its head. This principle of protection was of a dual nature. Not only would the animal or insect depicted protect the spirit of the deceased person but it would be unable to injure him for the hieroglyphic was drawn so that the lion would be depicted in two halves, the serpent with knives stabbing it, the bee minus its head as stated, and the viper cut in two with sand between the two halves to keep them apart.

The main idea behind these forms of talismans was that of a magical spell of a simple nature, embodying once again the principles of protection and of benefit. The same idea is maintained to the present day, for the wearing of charms and talismans is for the dual purpose of safeguarding against accident, disease, misfortune and the evil of other people, and for the attracting of brighter and happier conditions of an emotional, financial and material nature.

Closely linked with the history of talismans we find a great variety of amulets or charms which were in use among the Oriental nations from the most remote times.

Swastika

Perhaps the most ancient is that of the wheel and cross, which was in ancient days used by the Chinese and Hindus, and can, it is said, be traced to a former race of humanity in the Neolithic Age, engraved on stone implements of the period. Indeed, it is to be found in almost all the temples and ruins of the ancient world, and is in use even today among the more enlightened peoples of the West as a 'charm' for good fortune. Its name in the Sanscrit tongue means 'purveyor of good fortune' or, rather, 'well-being'. It is known as the Wheel of the Law, the law referred to being that of cyclic revolution or periodicity by which history is made to repeat itself in the necessary connection between Cause and Effect. It is a tacit affirmation of the fact that we reap what we sow, and that present effects are the direct fruit of past causes. In this sense it embodies the idea of the evolution of the human soul, by cyclic peregrination and experience. This ancient symbol is found to be cast on bells in several churches in Great Britain, and the fact that it is found all over the world argues for a common origin of which history has now lost all trace. The most common form of the Swastika is

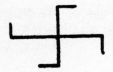

which is termed the 'Male' form. There is, however, the inverted form known as the 'Female' Swastika whose arms will be seen pointing in the opposite direction, that is to the left instead of to the right.

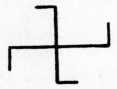

This was the form of Swastika used by the Hitlerite regime in Germany. It may well be that the using of the Swastika in this form helped to lay emphasis on the apparent idealisation of sex.

It should be pointed out that this reversed form of the Swastika is that commonly used in certain Black Magical rites.

The Tau

This symbol is in universal use as a sacred emblem, and is subjected to many variations of form. The simplest of these is the one formed by two straight lines, one being vertical and the other superposed upon it horizontally, like a block letter T.

To this form a handle is given by the Egyptians, making the figure of the Ankh, which word indicates the first person singular of the verb to be, and signifies 'I am'—that is, Living. Hence it is used as a symbol of Life, and was carried by all the Kings and Priests. It was used by St Anthony, the Copt hermit, for the cure of St Anthony's fire, or erysipelas, and inflammatory conditions of the skin. It was in great use among the Jews for this purpose and for epilepsy. Hence it comes about that this symbol is now known as St Anthony's Cross. The Brotherhood of St Anthony bear a badge on the right shoulder with the Tau symbol and the word 'Anthon'. Later in the history of this symbol of the Tau we find it elaborated to take a form known as the Triple Tau, which is formed thus:

The Fish

The symbol of the Fish has always been regarded as a sign of increase and wealth because of its remarkable fertility, and even in these days it is seen cut out of mother-of-pearl, and used as a charm or pendant for good fortune. In ancient days the worhip of Dagon, the Sun Fish, was prevalent among the Syrians, and may have given rise to the concept of the Mermaid.

The Fish symbol is not peculiar to the talismanic art of the Philistines, but has entered into the gnosis of the Hebrews, who may have adopted it during one of their lapses into idolatry. The name Dag is Hebrew for fish, and as Dagon it is suggested that the Sun was worshipped on its entry into the sign Pisces. As the Nun it is associated with the Vestal Virgins or Nuns, and is thus connected with Venus, the planet of fecundity or fruitfulness, allotted to Friday or *Dies Piscis*, Fish Day. It will be remembered that Joshua was the son of Nun, which has been regarded as the prototype of the birth of the Saviour of Israel by the issue from the first of the Order of the Immaculate.

The Scarab

The Scarabæus or Sacred Beetle was used as an amulet by the Egyptians, who regarded it as the symbol of the Creator, and most of the cartouches found in the ancient ruins of that once great centre of art and culture are faced by this symbol and the words, 'RA MEN KHEPHER', Ra, Creator of the Universe. The Khepher is thus indicated as the embodiment of the creative power of the Sun God, Ra. The symbol was derived from the sacred beetle, which deposited its eggs in balls of clay which the parent beetle rolled along. This action was suggestive of the passage of the sun in the heavens, the orb being as it were rolled like a ball round the earth. Moreover, it was the sun's heat that eventually hatched out the young beetle, and hence the sun was regarded as being invested with creative powers. The Scarab in green stone, inlaid with gold, was placed on the breast of deceased persons, or even embedded in their hearts during the process of embalming. This was deemed to be efficacious in protecting the dead from molestation by evil spirits on their way through the underworld. When we consider the action of the sun on the clay ball and the subsequent production of the living beetle we can see how this imagery of the Scarab applies to the man of clay, from which there is raised up by the action of the Spiritual Sun a living creature or Soul. The cartouche and the Scarab are here represented.

The Eye

This amulet or charm represents the Sun, which is spoken of as 'The Eye of Day,' and is symbolic of the

Supreme Intelligence, or the All-seeing Eye of the Deity. From being a circle with a point in the centre, which denotes the First Manifestation of the Divine Being, it was later made to take the form of an open eye, and as such was in general use as an amulet to forefend against evils of enchantment, enmity, and diseases of all kinds. A talisman, embodying the symbols of both the Sun and Moon, that is the left eye and the right eye together, was formed at the new Moon in Leo or Cancer, these being the signs of the Sun and Moon, when the Sun, being near the summer solstice, has its greatest strength, which it transfers to the Moon, so that a double source of protection and strength is invoked by this combination. Its simple form is thus represented:

Talismans of all kinds are to be found among the relics of the Greek, Etruscan, Gnostic, and other cults of art and learning. The Dove, the Lamb, the Fish, the Crown, the Tortoise, Lion, Unicorn, etc., have all been employed as symbols of efficacy in various directions, and in comparatively recent centuries have been in use on seals and finger-rings; but no people seem to have carried the talismanic art to the same degree of perfection as did the Hebrew Kabalists and Thaumaturgists, and for this reason more particular attention has been given in these pages to the exposition of the Hebraic cult.

A study of these ancient beliefs and symbols leads directly to a consideration of the possibility of a sort of universal conflict between the powers of Light and Darkness, the existence and efficacy of Good and Evil spirits in the world, and the more controversial question of humanity's freedom and of the power of the individual soul in the universe. These questions may now be answered from the point of view of Kabalistic teachings.

Other kinds of talismans are depicted in the form of flies, and necklaces were made of them. The fly is an emblem of activity and swiftness and in the old days was often worn by travellers so as to help them to get from place to place as quickly as possible and in safety. Today, the fly would be used more as a talisman in connection with air travel, this being the swiftest form of modern travel.

Talismans in the form of crescents come under the influence of the Moon and are used as a protection against the evil eye and witchery, but can also be used for the advancing of personal and material interests of life. Particular care should, however, be observed as to the way the points of the crescent are pointing. These should always point to the left—☽—as this then becomes the symbol of the First Quarter of the Moon, the Quarter between New Moon and Full Moon or the Quarter of Increase, when things develop and prosper.

The Crescent should never be made or worn with the points pointing towards the right— ☾ —for this is the symbol of the third or Last Quarter of the Moon when it is going from Full Moon to New Moon and is decreasing in power and losing its strength. To wear such a form of crescent would only be to interfere with one's progress.

The crescent is particularly helpful for all matters to do with children and young people and for those commencing new activities and interests.

The Counterpoise of Collar (*Menet*) is a symbolic talisman. It is associated with the zodiacal sign of Taurus and the planet Venus. It brings joy and health. Venus is the planet of Love, Life and Laughter and this Talisman will help forward True Love, will strengthen the vitality and the resistance to illness and will bring many social pleasures and activities.

Leopard's Claw: Although the modern interpretation is that this form of talisman is worn for protection against wild animals, the original usage of this was a form of recognition and hence as a protection. Men, and sometimes women, in certain tribes, who had studied the magical art, were reputed to be able to turn themselves into leopards and thus the more easily destroy their enemies and those whom they disliked. In later times this degenerated into the men or women concerned wearing the skin of a leopard and having specially prepared claws made which could cover their hands and literally enable them to tear their victims to pieces.

Yet in order that they should recognise other Leopard-men, and be recognised themselves as Leopard-men, the emblem of the leopard's claw was created and the wearing of this would ensure safety. This symbol of protection and safety could also be conferred on certain others of the tribe who were friends, or for services rendered or to be rendered.

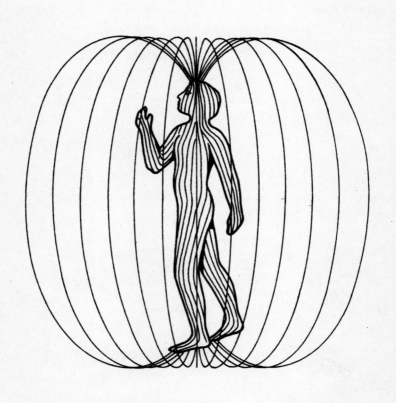

CHAPTER 5

MAKING TALISMANS

The basis of all talismans is the circle. This can be drawn on parchment or paper, or engraved on a particular metal. The parchment, paper or metal can be either round or square.

Reference to the Pentacle of Rabbi Solomon the King, shown on page 79, will reveal that this talisman consists of an outer circle of double lines and three inner circles of single lines. Between these lines are various names and Hebrew hieroglyphs. In the centre of these circles is a combination of two six-pointed stars which represent the Seal of Solomon and two five-pointed stars or Pentacles which, in magic, represent the symbol of The Man. Therefore these interlaced stars, six-pointed and five-pointed, represent Solomon as both King and Man. At each point of these interlaced stars there is what appears to be the top part of a Cross and between these there are other symbols. The top part of the Cross and the symbols between are in reality a condensed form of what is known as the sigil of the planet under whose influence the talisman is made.

It will be noticed that these various talismans can only be made on certain days of the week and the particular day on which they are made must be the day ruled by the planet which has power over the talisman or, alternatively, when it is stated that a talisman can be made on a specific day then the Sigil of the Planet ruling that day must be incorporated in the centre design. A third alternative is that when, as in the case of the Pentacle of Rabbi Solomon the King, it is stated that it can be made on any day of the week except Saturday, then the sigil of the planet ruling the day on which it is actually made should be incorporated in the centre design. If the talisman should be made on a Tuesday then the sigil of Mars should be used and if on a Thursday then the sigil of Jupiter and so on.

To refresh readers' memories and to avoid any possibility of error the days of the week and their planetary rulers are as follows:

Sunday	Sun	☉
Monday	Moon	☽
Tuesday	Mars	♂
Wednesday	Mercury	☿
Thursday	Jupiter	♃
Friday	Venus	♀
Saturday	Saturn	♄

On page 76, is given a series of diagrams showing the component parts of the Pentacle of Rabbi Solomon the King. The Magic Circle is shown separately with various names between the inner circles—these are the names of deities whose influence is invoked to make the Pentacle (or talisman) of powerful import and the names of the deities must again conform to the day of the week on which the Pentacle or talisman is made.

A Table of these deities, the days they rule, the full sigil of the planet ruling the day together with the symbol of the planet and the sign or signs ruled by the planet are given on page 77.

To return to our description of the component parts of the Pentacle of Rabbi Solomon illustrated on page 76, the two diagrams on each side of the Magic Circle are known as the Intelligence of the planet and are sometimes incorporated in the seal of the planet used on the obverse side of some of the talismans or made separately and carried in the same receptacle as the talisman.

An illustration of the Magic Ring of Solomon is given below the Magic Circle and should be made of Gold. Instead of a precious stone being set in the ring, a six-pointed star is engraved similarly to a signet ring. A small Pentagram or five-pointed star is illustrated and also a large six-pointed star termed the Pentacle of Solomon. Two of each of these are incorporated in the centre diagram of Rabbi Solomon.

The drawing beneath the five-pointed star is an illustration of another form of sigil that can be used in a talisman. The remaining illustration is a form of Magic Wand.

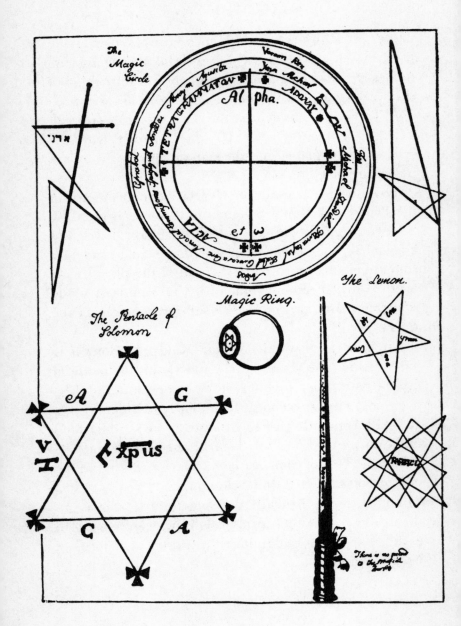

The Magic Circle

Alpha.

et ω

Magic Ring.

The Pentacle of Solomon

A   G

V
H   xpus

G   A

The Lemon.

There is no point to the Magic Knife

76

A Table shewing the names of the Angels governing the 7 days of the week
with their Sigils, Planets, Signs, &c.

Sunday	Monday	Tuesday	Wednesday	Thursday	Friday	Saturday
Michāel	Gabriel	Camael	Raphāel	Sachiel	Anāel	Caffiel
name of the 4ᵗʰ Heaven	name of the 1ˢᵗ Heaven	name of the 5ᵗʰ Heaven	name of the 2ⁿᵈ Heaven	name of the 6ᵗʰ Heaven	name of the 3ʳᵈ Heaven	No Angels ruling above the 6ᵗʰ Heaven
Machen.	Shamain.	Machon.	Raqure.	Zebul.	Sagun.	

THE PENTACLE OF RABBI SOLOMON THE KING

This Pentacle can be made any day in the week except Saturday. It is said to be a most necessary talisman to have when evoking spirits, and also is very efficacious for all good; so much so that the most evil genii cannot injure the person wearing it when it is present. It should, however, be worn with the corresponding seals as shown on pages 83 and 85.

Nevertheless, although this talisman and the corresponding seals, can be made on any day but a Saturday, there are certain parts of each day which are more efficacious for its making than others.

Each day has a specific planetary ruler and each hour of the day also has a sub-planetary ruler. The 1st, 8th, 15th and 22nd hours of each day are ruled by the planet ruling that day and these hours are the best hours for the making of the talisman and seals.

If preferred, the talismans and seals can be cut out from the pages in this chapter (providing the reader does not mind mutilating the book) and placed in a silk bag for carrying on one's person so as to obtain the full effects of their influences; but they should be cut out and placed in the silk bag on the day and in the appropriate hour in accordance with the instructions for making each talisman and seal.

THE MOST SACRED SEALS OF RABBI SOLOMON THE KING

I.

The above seal is worn as companion to No. II, which is shown on page 85; but when only one seal is used with the Pentacle it is recommended that this seal should be chosen. It should, however, be quite understood that it is much better that both be worn, in accordance with ancient custom.

For illustration of the Pentacle see page 79.

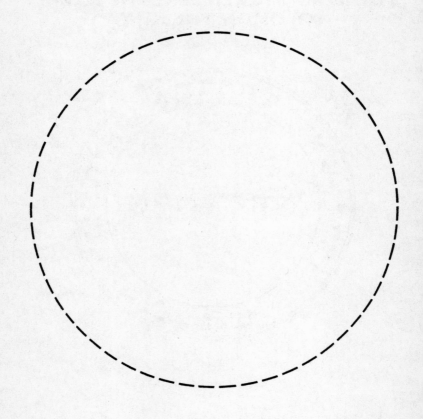

Template for cutting out the seal on the previous page.

THE MOST SACRED SEALS OF RABBI SOLOMON THE KING

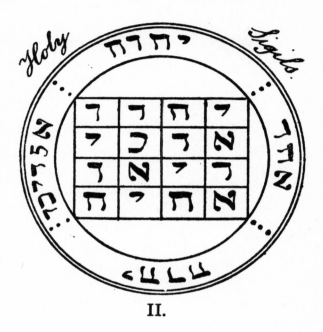

II.

The above Seal is one of two which are usually worn in conjunction with the Pentacle of Rabbi Solomon. It is best to have both of them; but they can be used separately if desired. The ancients placed the utmost faith in these sacred seals, especially in connection with the Rabbi Solomon Pentacle.

For illustration of the other seal see page 83, and of the Pentacle see page 79.

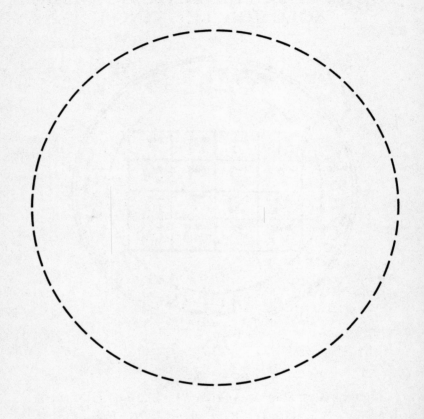

Template for cutting out the seal on the previous page.

Although the Pentacle of Rabbi Solomon the King with its accompanying seal or seals is necessary for the evoking of spirits and for all good, it is, in the first respect more applicable for use by those interested in magic itself or in the investigation of psychic matters or the developing of the psychic faculties.

In the second instance the term 'efficacious for all good' is very broad in its over-all meaning. It can apply to people whose activities and efforts are devoted to the welfare of others, such as doctors, surgeons, nurses, etc.; as well as to those who are associated with any form of religion, or to those who seek to help persons who have fallen into wrong ways of life and who have suffered accordingly.

In each instance there is a need for discrimination as to the particular day on which the Talisman, Seal or Seals should be made or cut out from the book. The specific ruling is any day of the week *except Saturday*. This naturally implies from Sunday to Friday and hence it is of importance to choose the right day.

Sunday should be used for making or cutting out this talisman and the seal or seals, by those who occupy authoritative and influential positions and who exercise authority over others. People in short who are at the head of affairs in their own particular line of activity. For those who may wish to make the talisman, if made on this day the metal should be of gold.

Monday should be used by people holding lesser positions of an administrative nature, those who take orders from others in higher positions or from the head of the firm or organisation, but who can also give orders or instructions to others. If actually making the talisman and seal or seals, they should be made of silver.

Tuesday should be used by doctors and surgeons, nurses and all others who administer to the general health of others, for Tuesday is ruled by Mars and this is the planet of medicine, surgery and all associated activities. For those who wish to make the talisman, etc., the metal iron should be used.

Wednesday should be used by those who have to do with mental health, the psychiatrists, etc., the psychologists, the manipulative healers such as osteopaths, and those who practise natural therapies. In addition, all whose activities embrace the giving of practical advice for the good and benefit of other people can cut out or make this particular talisman on this day. In making it, silver, platinum or aluminium should be used.

Thursday should be used by all associated with religion and with any form of missionary work, as well as with charitable and philanthropic interests. Sometimes legal interests, where the effort, advice and action are associated with welfare and kindred matters, can be influenced by the making of the talisman and seals on this day, or if the talisman is cut out on this day. If made, the metal used should be tin.

Friday should be used where financial interests associated with all or any of the interests previously described are concerned. Alternatively it is a day when matters specifically connected with women can be influenced, for the planet Venus has rule over this day and Venus is a feminine planet. If the talisman is actually made, the metal used should be copper.

A TALISMAN FOR THE FRUITS OF THE EARTH

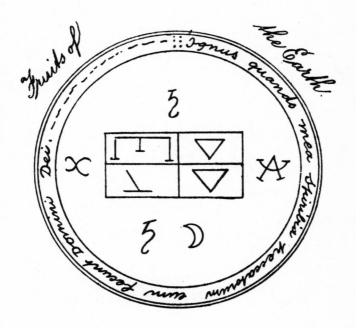

This talisman should be made on a Saturday, when Saturn is in conjunction with Jupiter or Venus, or in good aspect to Mercury. It is said to be a splendid talisman for farmers, cattle dealers, estate agents, poultry farmers, etc.

The corresponding seal which should be worn with this talisman is shown on page 93.

91

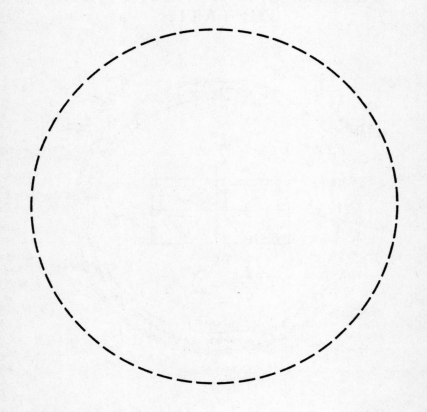

Template for cutting out the talisman on the previous page. It should be made on a Saturday when Saturn is in conjunction with Jupiter or Venus, or in good aspect to Mercury.

THE GREAT SEAL OF THE FRUITS OF THE EARTH

This seal should be used in conjunction with the talisman to which it belongs, as illustrated on page 91. The wearing of this, together with the talisman, is said to make the charm doubly efficacious.

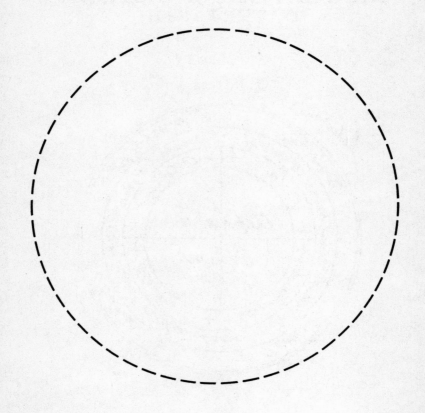

Template for cutting out the seal on the previous page, for use in conjunction with the talisman to which it belongs.

The Talisman for the Fruits of the Earth should be made on a Saturday in accord with the planetary instructions given on page 91.

For those who desire to actually make this Talisman, the metal used should be lead which comes under the influence of the planet Saturn, and according to the convenience of the person making it, during the first, eighth, fifteenth or twenty-second hours of the day.

If the reader wishes to cut this talisman and seal out of the book in preference to making it then they should only be cut out on a Saturday in one of the hours specified.

It is specifically favourable for farmers, cattle dealers, poultry farmers, horticulturists, floriculturists, market gardeners, estate agents, etc.

In addition, all persons who are in any way connected with mining, but coal-mining in particular, irrespective of their actual position in the industry, can use this talisman for the furthering of their legitimate interests.

A TALISMAN TO SECURE ELOQUENCE

This talisman should be made on a Wednesday. It is said to aid one in learning and public speaking, and should be worn by clergymen, auctioneers, politicians, etc.

The corresponding seal for use with this talisman is shown on page 99.

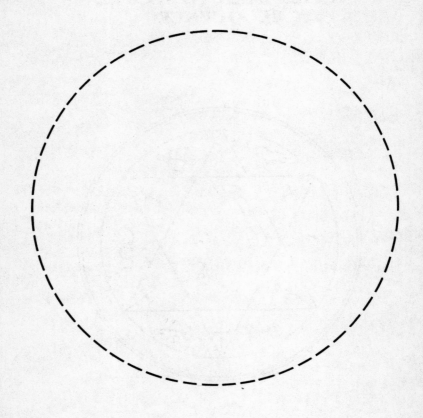

Template for cutting out the talisman on the previous page. It should be made on a Wednesday.

THE SEAL OF ELOQUENCE

The Seal of Mercury belongs by ancient custom to the Talisman of Eloquence, which is illustrated on page 97. It is said that those who desire to become orators and successful public speakers find great benefit from the use of these in combination.

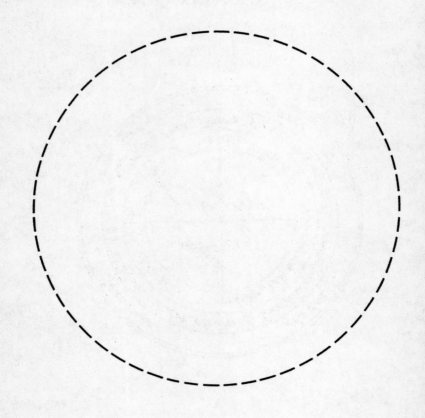

Template for cutting out the seal on the previous page.

As stated on page 97, the Talisman to Secure Eloquence together with its seal should be made on a Wednesday if it is desired to make it, and it should be made of silver, platinum or aluminium in either the first, eighth, fifteenth or twenty-second hour of the day.

Alternatively for readers who wish to cut out the talisman and seal and place in a silk bag for safe carrying this should be done on a Wednesday in one of the hours specified.

The talisman will assist all those who are desirous of becoming writers, authors, journalists, orators and who may wish to develop ability for radio, television, stage or screen activities.

Concentration upon this talisman will intensify the natural inspiration and hence assist in the writing of books and plays, poetry or short stories.

In addition to the above, the wearing of the talisman will help to promote safety in travel and will protect all those who work on the railway, in the air or who have any connection whatsoever with transport and travel.

A TALISMAN FOR HONOUR AND RICHES

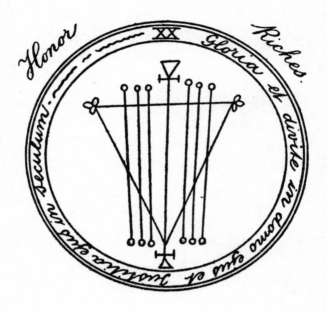

This Pentacle should be made on a Sunday, and is said to raise a person to honour and dignity; also it helps a person to become rich, and should be worn by people holding high positions, those on the stock exchange, bankers, and in all kinds of business; also those who want to improve their position or business.

The corresponding seal for use with this talisman is shown on page 105.

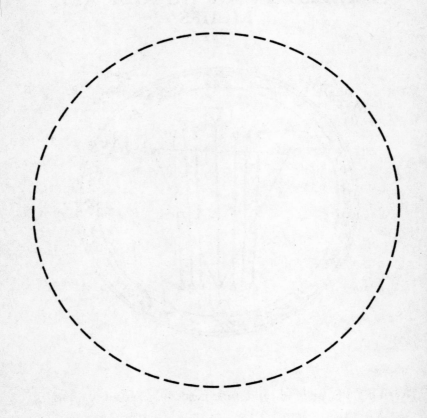

*Template for cutting out the talisman on the
previous page. It should be made on a Sunday.*

THE SEAL OF GREAT PROSPERITY

The above seal may be used in combination with any one of the talismans shown on pages 103, 109 and 117. Its use is said to greatly enhance the value of the talisman with which it is worn.

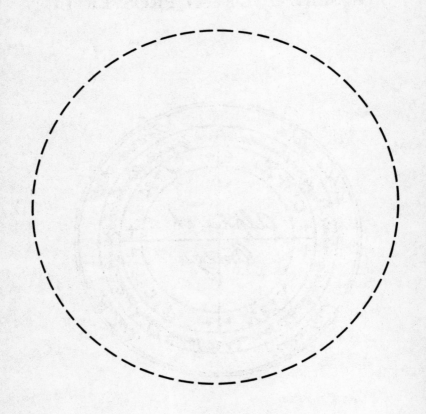

Template for cutting out the seal shown on the
previous page.

The Talisman for Honour and Riches together with its seal should be made on a Sunday and, if metal is desired, should be made of gold.

Those readers wishing to cut out the talisman and seal should do so on a Sunday in the first, eighth, fifteenth or twenty-second hour according to convenience, and place them in a silken bag.

All those who are ambitious should certainly carry this talisman and seal as its influence will enable them to make the right contacts, and to say and do the correct things at the right time, and will help to lift them from mediocrity to relative eminence.

For those who already occupy high positions, this talisman and seal will ensure continuity of their established place and safeguard against the attacks of open or secret enemies.

This talisman and seal are designed for all who desire honour and riches in whatever sphere of activity they may find themselves.

A TALISMAN FOR HEALTH

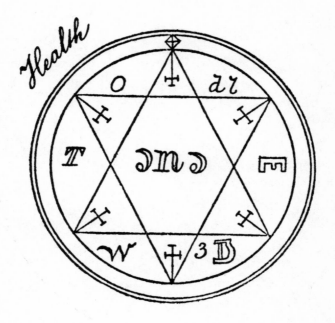

This should be made on a Sunday, and is said to be a wonderful preservative for health, also for curing diseases. All persons suffering should wear one; even when in health it is well to possess one.

For the corresponding seal for use with this talisman see page 105.

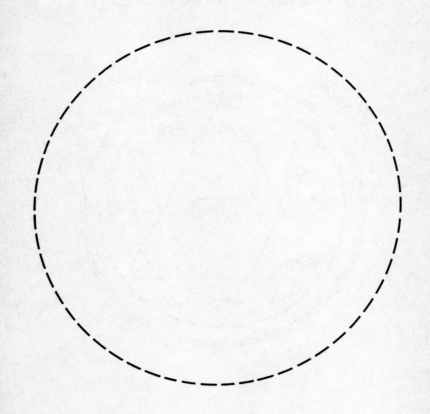

Template for cutting out the talisman shown on the previous page. It should be made on a Sunday.

110

The Talisman for Health and its seal should be made or cut out of the book on a Sunday. If made it should be made of Gold. The reason for doing this on a Sunday is that this day is ruled by the Sun and this luminary governs the vitality and life force. It should be made or cut out in the 1st, 8th, 15th or 22nd hour of the day.

Not only is this a very powerful talisman for the preserving and maintaining of good health by people generally, it is also extremely helpful for all persons who are associated in any way with the art of healing.

Doctors and surgeons, and nurses should wear it for it will assist them in their good work. It will also aid those who follow nature cure methods, manipulation and spiritual healing, as its possession will help both diagnosis and practice.

As an alternative, doctors, physicians, nurses and all whose activities are what may be termed 'bloodless' could make this talisman on a Thursday, or cut it out of the book on Thursday and place it in a silk bag as suggested, for this day comes under the influence of Jupiter which is the healing planet. The same hours as for Sunday should be used.

For surgeons, dentists and others, veterinary surgeons included, Tuesday would be an alternative day to Sunday as this day is ruled by Mars, the planet that rules any form of surgery. If made, it should be made of iron. The same hours as for Sunday should be used.

Again, as an alternative, Tuesday could be used by all persons connected with machinery, such as engin-

eers, toolmakers, ship-builders, road and railway con-
structors and so on, as they too, come under the
influence of the planet Mars.

Soldiers and sailors would find this talisman very
effective if made on a Tuesday or cut out on a Tuesday
in preference to a Sunday.

A TALISMAN FOR TRAVELLING BY LAND OR SEA

This talisman should be made on a Monday, and is said to be good for people who travel by land or sea, short or long journeys.

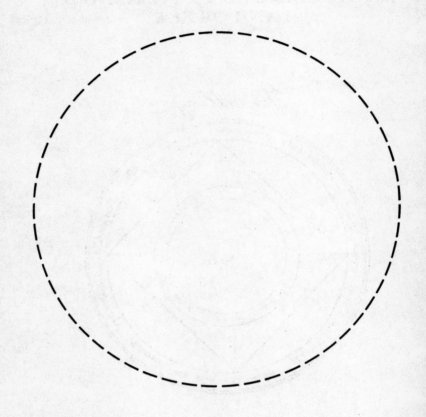

Template for cutting out the talisman shown on the previous page. It should be made on a Monday.

The Talisman for Travelling on Land or Sea does not require an accompanying seal. As stated it should be made on a Monday, of silver, or cut out from the book on a Monday, the 1st, 8th, 15th and 22nd hours being the requisite hours for either of these purposes.

The talisman can be made either to cover general travel or for a specific journey and is very helpful if a long distance overseas journey is contemplated or should emigration to another country be in prospect.

Hence it does not matter what particular walk of life a person may be in or what their occupation is; this talisman will be helpful in smoothing out difficulties in the arranging of travel; it will help to make the journey that is taken safe and pleasant and it will bring contact with travelling companions of a helpful and cheerful nature.

From a specific standpoint it should certainly be worn by all those who are directly connected with travel. Train drivers and guards should certainly wear it, and signalmen too. All those who hold any position on board ship from commodores and captains down to waiters and stokers should wear it as it will assist from the safety standpoint, will help to prevent sea-sickness and will cause the ordinary work to seem less arduous.

A TALISMAN FOR ALL KINDS OF PROSPERITY

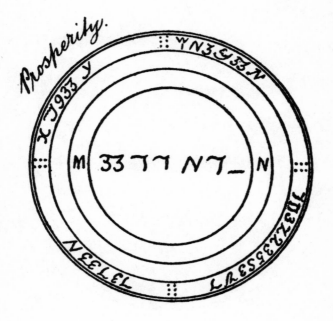

This talisman should be made on a Sunday, and is very good for business people and all traders to wear.

For the corresponding seal for use with this talisman see page 105.

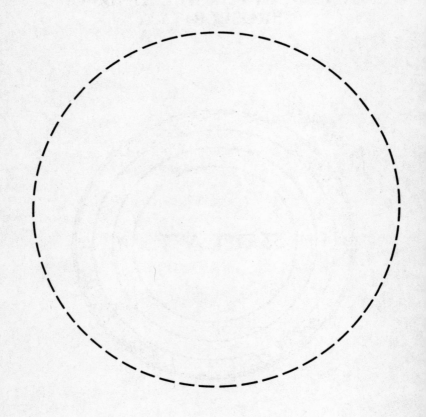

Template for cutting out the talisman shown on the previous page. It should be made on a Sunday.

The Talisman for All Kinds of Prosperity although designed more specifically for business people and traders can be worn by persons in other lines of activity in order to increase their general prosperity.

For those who wish to make it, it should be made on a Sunday, together with its seal, and should be made of gold, but for those who wish to cut the talisman and seal out of the book then it should be cut out on a Sunday, in either the 1st, 8th, 15th or 22nd hour.

The term 'business people' naturally covers a wide variety of interests and it does not necessarily mean that you must be the 'boss' or the managing director. You can be in an executive position, big or small; you can help in the serving of produce, it does not matter, the wearing of this talisman will help to increase your general prosperity.

Traders also cover a wide variety of activities inclusive of food and merchandise and the wearing of this talisman will help them in salesmanship whether it be in the selling of an airliner or ship, or the selling of a pound of tomatoes in the market place.

A TALISMAN FOR TRADE

This talisman should be made on a Thursday, and is said to be helpful to those engaged in any kind of business and particularly, in combination with its seal, for activities of a speculative nature.

The corresponding seal for use with this talisman is shown on page 123.

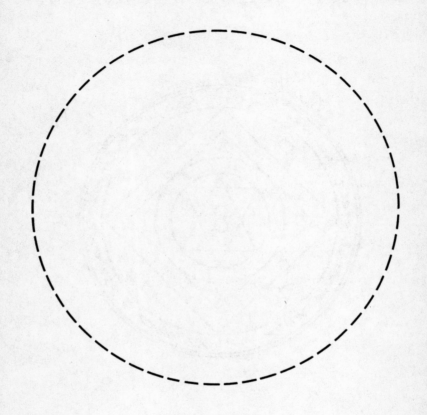

Template for cutting out the talisman shown on the previous page. It should be made on a Thursday.

THE SEAL OF TRADE AND HAZARD

The Seal of Jupiter is said to be one of the greatest
assets anyone engaged in trade or other employment of a
speculative nature can possibly have. Used in connection with the Talisman for Trade shown on page 121, it
is said to be a wonderful aid to success.

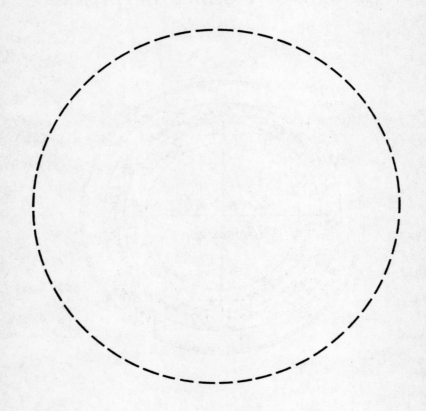

Template for cutting out the talisman shown on the previous page.

The Talisman for Trade and its seal apply to business and trading activities in a very broad sense and can be worn by people in many differing spheres of life.

As stated on page 121, it should be made on a Thursday. It should be made of tin, but it can also be cut out on a Thursday in the 1st, 8th, 15th or 22nd hour of the day.

In addition, the use of this talisman with its seal is favourable for speculation and investment. At the same time individual preference and choice are essential, and common sense should be used.

The majority of people today know something of football, horse and dog racing and can weigh up the practical possibilities, but if you are more interested in one of these than in the others then the talisman should be applied to the particular sport in which you are interested as by concentration upon it your choice and power of selection will be enhanced.

The same applies to investments. If you know nothing of the stock markets, then concentration on your talisman will aid you in choosing the financial adviser who will make reasonable and helpful suggestions as to the stocks and shares you should take up.